DATE DUE			

Homeless Children

Look for these and other books in the Lucent Overview series:

Homeless Children

by Karen O'Connor

LUCENT
B·O·O·K·S

LUCENT Overview Series

Library of Congress Cataloging-in-Publication Data

O'Connor, Karen, 1938-
  Homeless children / by Karen O'Connor.
    p. cm. — (Lucent overview series)
  Includes bibliographical references.
  Summary: Discusses the causes and prevention of homelessness
and what is being done to help solve this problem.
  ISBN 1-56006-109-X
  1. Homelessness—United States—Juvenile literature. 2. Socially
handicapped children—United States—Juvenile literature.
[1. Homelessness. 2. Homeless persons.] I. Title. II. Series.
HV4505.026 1989
362.7'08'6942—dc20   89-37553
                                                                         CIP
                                                                          AC

To Stephanie
for caring
for the homeless child in me

"Children should not be bought and sold. They should not be exploited. It should not be unspeakably dangerous for a kid to be alone and homeless on the streets of our cities."

Father Bruce Ritter
Covenant House, New York, New York

Contents

CHAPTER ONE

No Place to Call Home

Eleven-year-old Pete* and his thirty-six-year-old mother, Ellen, camp out regularly. Not in the mountains or on the beach however—they sleep under a bridge in the downtown area of a West Coast city. They share one thin blanket on a bed of cardboard. Homelessness "really scares me," Pete told a reporter for a local newspaper. "It's an adventure I'm ready to see end."

Pete and his mother moved from their midwestern home hoping for a better life. They are still hoping. "I don't like sleeping out like this," said shaggy-haired Pete. "One night we saw a guy get hit in the head with a metal pipe."

In Tennessee, Lois and her two preschool children were forced out of their home after a broken marriage. With little money and an old car, Lois worried about how she would care for her baby and young son. For awhile they lived in her Dodge Colt.

While the children slept, their mother stayed awake. "I was too scared to fall asleep," she said. "More than anything, I want a safe place for my kids."

Worry and fear are common emotions among the homeless of any age. But parents with children carry additional burdens. How will they keep their children safe? How will they feed their children? How will the children get an education?

*Author's Note: The names of the young people in this book have been changed and their stories disguised to protect their identities.

Most homeless people today, more than at any time in U.S. history, are ordinary people who have fallen upon hard times. "Skid-row bums" are no longer the only people who roam the streets and sleep under bridges. The homeless are the jobless workers who got fired because of budget cuts or other problems. They are the unemployed who did not have work benefits. They are part of the millions of people who work for minimum wage. They are the people on the waiting list for public housing. They are refugees from other nations. They are veterans who went away to war and came home sick or wounded and ended up homeless. They are the children who live with these homeless people. Or they are the children who have either run away from their homes or have been kicked out of their homes.

Three million homeless in America

Although it is impossible to count accurately the number of homeless people in America, experts estimate that up to three million people do not have homes. The number increases every year.

The National Coalition for the Homeless estimates that there are at least 70,000 homeless in New York; 50,000 in Los Angeles; 25,000 in Chicago; 4,000-14,000 in Dallas; 10,000-15,000 in Washington, D.C.; 10,000 in Miami; and 6,500 in Phoenix. Among the homeless are over one million children.

Homelessness is increasing in numbers. It also includes a wider range of the population. A picture of the homeless, nationwide, resembles a family portrait.

About 30 percent are families with children.
About 50 percent are single men.
About 14 percent are single women.
About 20-30 percent are employed.
About 40 percent are veterans.
About 30 percent are children without families.

The New York City shelter system houses more than 5,000 families, including 13,000 children, half of whom are under six years of age.

Other cities (such as Charleston, South Carolina; Philadelphia, Pennsylvania; Los Angeles, California; and Providence, Rhode Island) report increasing numbers of homeless families with young children.

In New York City, 76 percent of the homeless are families with children, and in Boston the figure is 67 percent. They make up 50 percent in Philadelphia, Pennsylvania; Trenton, New Jersey; and Yonkers, New York.

There are many reasons why people suddenly find themselves without a home.

Lack of affordable housing—From 1977 through 1981 the federal government authorized more than forty thousand units of new public

Homeless families are sometimes forced to live in their cars or vans because shelters are overcrowded. Although many homeless people are employed, they still cannot afford the high costs of housing.

housing each year. These housing projects were built for people who had little money to spend on homes. However, from 1982 through 1986, the number of units built dropped to less than five thousand. During those same years, homelessness increased dramatically.

Unemployment—A study conducted by the U.S. Congress revealed that high unemployment and low wages were the factors most responsible for the increase of poor and homeless Americans. In 1979, 460,000 people were unemployed for over six months. By 1982, this number had risen to 1.4 million. Four years later, it had dropped only slightly to 1.2 million.

But jobs alone do not solve the problem of homelessness. Eight million new jobs were created between 1979 and 1984. But more than half of them paid less than seven thousand dollars per year. This is well below the poverty line (11.2 thousand dollars per year)—the minimum income needed for a family of four to survive in the United States today.

The minimum wage, set at 3.35 dollars an hour, has not been increased since 1981. Yet the cost of living has risen by 33 percent. In addition, most low-paying jobs do not provide much-needed benefits such as health and disability insurance.

Cutback in federal programs—Government funds to help the poor, such as aid for families with children and the food stamp program, were also cut back during the eighties. As a result, many poor and marginally poor families have been forced to choose between buying food and paying rent.

Almost anyone can become homeless

Homelessness brings ruin: physically through loss of home and possessions, and emotionally through the breakdown of ties to family and community. And almost anyone can become homeless. Some researchers believe that many Americans are just a paycheck or two from disaster. They spend their money as fast as they earn it. For example, if a father loses his job or a family member is struck by

A mother and her children fight to save their home. Low-income housing in many cities is being replaced or refurbished to appeal to people who have more money to spend on rent. This forces many poor people out of their homes.

a life-threatening illness or accident, it would not take long for a family's savings to disappear.

Without sufficient income, parents could not pay rent and the family would be forced to move out. Without an address, the adults could not get a job easily. Without work, they would not have money to provide for their families. And without work benefits or help from government agencies, parents and children would end up on the street or roam from one shelter to another.

Fewer choices

At one time, people who found they could no longer afford to pay for their houses could move to a less expensive house. "It used to be families could survive by moving into a smaller house or by moving into a less desirable neighborhood," said Frank Landerville of the

San Diego Regional Task Force on the Homeless. But in most cities, there is simply nowhere to go.

In the past, the poor and homeless could usually move into hotels with single rooms to rent, boardinghouses, or low-rent apartments in the downtown area of big cities. But in recent years, many cities are improving and upgrading the tenement areas where most poor people lived. They are making these areas attractive to people with more money to spend on homes.

To meet the housing needs of the poor, directors of private and city shelters and church groups are looking at ways to extend their care. Many are now providing temporary housing, counseling, and meals for a month or more. But the housing problem is far from solved.

Mothers and young children

Homelessness is difficult enough for families that are intact—where parents and children are together. But those who are hit hardest are single mothers with young children.

According to the National Coalition for the Homeless in Washington, D.C., mothers and their children from birth to age ten are now the fastest growing segment of homeless people in the United States. This report is based on observations by people who serve the homeless in shelters and soup kitchens in all parts of the United States.

Many of these mothers simply are fleeing husbands or boyfriends who have neglected, abused, or abandoned them. They are frightened, worried, and confused about what to do next. Most of them do not have job skills because they depended on men to take care of them.

"Some of them have given up all that is secure," said Bill Molina of the Salvation Army. "They have no job, no day care, no family to turn to, and often have to rely on welfare."

In addition, homeless women and children do not always come forward for the care that is available. Many homeless mothers are hiding their children in order to protect them from abusive husbands and boyfriends. Some spend their nights under a bridge, in their cars, or in a cheap motel.

Twenty-four-year-old Jeannie, for example, tried to keep herself and her two daughters together in one room of an abandoned farmhouse after leaving an abusive boyfriend. But the place had no indoor plumbing, no running water, and minimum electricity.

Jeannie and her daughters walked or hitchhiked for miles each week to get a hot meal at a soup kitchen. Without a permanent address, they did not qualify for public assistance. They lived this way for eight months until a social worker helped them move into a temporary shelter.

Cardboard cartons become temporary homes for transients sleeping outside a mission in Los Angeles. Because of its warm climate, Southern California is "home" to many homeless people in winter.

A small child in New York examines what remains of an apartment building. Some of New York's condemned buildings are being renovated to house the homeless. However, thirteen thousand homeless children in New York continue to live in shelters.

According to Norma Rossi, a volunteer for the National Coalition for the Homeless, a lost puppy is often treated better than a homeless child. "When someone finds a puppy on the curb, he can take it to the pound where it will get food and shelter for the night," said Rossi. "But when it's a homeless parent with a child, there are times when no agency has room to take them in. They are set loose alone on the street. That's less than humane."

More than homeless

It is important to look at the effects of homelessness on children. For children, homelessness involves a whole lot more than the absence of a permanent place to live. Boys and girls who grow up without a home suffer from improper diets, low self-esteem, bed-wetting, speech impediments, lack of schooling, behavioral problems, and emotional damage that can last a lifetime.

The Harvard Medical School conducted a survey of 210 homeless children in Massachusetts and found that nearly half were behind in language, social, and coordination skills. One two-year-old child could not walk yet. Others had problems talking clearly or staying dry through the night.

Also, homeless children are frequently noisy and unruly. "It's not that they're bad," reported one shelter director, Paul Watson. "But the parents are short-tempered and stressed out, and the kids haven't had enough of a stable environment to know how to act."

Children need the comfort and stability of a place called home. They require friends and activities that are appropriate for their age and interests. Playing, socializing, and attending school without long-term interruptions are necessary to a healthy growing-up childhood.

But for homeless children these are distant dreams. Daily life for a child without a permanent home and a regular classroom is a life of chaos. Most cannot depend on anything. Clothing is usually secondhand and ill-fitting. Food received in food lines is often tasteless and cold. Friends are left behind because of frequent moves. Parents are usually too stressed and worried to give their children the time and nurturing they require. Toys, games, and stuffed animals are rare and ball games, piano lessons, and birthday parties are often nonexistent.

Being a child with no place to call home must be considered one of childhood's most devastating experiences.

Homeless and alone

Homeless young adults have different problems than homeless children. Most are old enough to survive on their own, but too young to qualify for public assistance. Many are in hiding from abusive

Mothers and their young children are the fastest growing group of homeless in America. Many of these mothers are battered wives who have left abusive husbands.

parents, the law, school authorities, and probation officers. To turn to a shelter or social worker would mean exposure. To stay alive, many turn to drug dealing or prostitution. Some become pregnant and end up on welfare. Below several young adults describe their lives on the street.

Peddling drugs from a bicycle

One eleven-year-old dropout, for example, earned two hundred dollars a day peddling drugs from his bicycle. Instead of thinking about homework, after-school sports, or Boy Scouts, as many boys his age do, Lenny had his mind on a fast car and a high-powered .38 caliber gun.

Seventeen-year-old "Crack" said he is not afraid of jail or the death penalty. "I'd been on the streets so long that I carried a gun wherever I went, even in school."

Sixteen-year-old Lana oversees a brood of thirteen children. A mix of family and friends, these children are the offspring of Lana's mother and sister—both dead—and those of a homeless family friend.

Lana is homeless too. For the time being, she and the children cram together in her grandmother's apartment in a seedy New Orleans public-housing project called "Desire."

Lana's life does not appear much different from other teens who are homeless and alone. Her mother died a drug addict. And Lana's father is in jail. Lana dreams of buying a designer dress and growing up pretty and getting out of the project someday.

Rachel did not live long enough to realize her dream of marrying a rich man and owning a big house. At age nineteen, she sat down in front of a church and put a bullet through her head. But before that final day, she had found a home among the homeless, in the pit of violence, drugs, and despair that exists in New York City's Grand Central Station. She felt free there, free from a broken family, free from drug treatment centers, and free from counselors who wanted to help her straighten out her life.

People who knew her said she was a sweet girl. She was known for doing little caring things for the battered and hardened adults who lived in the underground railroad station. But Rachel got hooked on cocaine. And one day when she could not get the money she needed for a fix, she ended her life.

A spark of hope

Not all kids like Lenny, Crack, Lana, and Rachel remain lost. Some actually make it. When they do, it's a testimony to the human spirit, to the kids themselves, and to the people who were committed to helping them.

Many live long enough to realize their dream. They leave the streets for school and jobs and family. For some, a job is the first step. "Many of these kids just want the opportunity to do something," said Herman Collins of the Triple Crown counseling center in Southern California. Without meaningful work, they turn to drugs and prostitution in order to survive.

For others, a loving home environment is the first step to recovery after years of intense abuse. One young man spent the first few years of his life in an abusive home. He was then placed in a loving foster home, where he recovered from his early years of abuse. He went to high school and then found a job taking care of the handicapped.

The downward spiral

Millions of American adults have escaped the cycle of poverty, abuse, and homelessness during the past twenty years. But at the same time, millions of children have entered that same cycle. According to the U.S. Census Bureau, one of every five American children lives in poverty—17 percent of white children, 40 percent of Hispanic children, and 50 percent of all black children.

According to a 1986 report in *Newsweek* magazine, this downward spiral is moving even faster for the youngest Americans: "An infant

These young children were left homeless after the city health department condemned the hotel they were living in. They have no where else to go, so they are living in the offices of the human resources administrator.

born today has nearly a one-in-four chance of starting life in a poor household.'' And homelessness often accompanies poverty.

The roots of poverty and homelessness go deep. Some experts believe that the cutting of government aid to the poor by 36.5 billion dollars during the eighties made things worse. ''We have taken very vulnerable families and knocked the pins out of them,'' said California Congressman George Miller. ''In many cases, they are working families or farm families who never thought they would ever be poor.''

There are no easy solutions to homelessness. In fact, there may still be more questions than answers. But the questions at least suggest that more people are aware of the homeless than ever before. And most agree that something needs to be done about their condition.

In a *New York Times*/CBS News Poll conducted in January 1989, most people interviewed said they wanted the government to be more involved in solving the homeless problem. Half said they'd be willing to pay higher taxes to help.

In 1986 and again in 1989, people were asked if they personally see homeless people around their community or on the way to work, or have they only read about these people or seen them on television? In 1986, 36 percent said they personally saw homeless people. In 1989, that figure had risen to 51 percent.

Perhaps the most important question, then, is whether we turn caring and compassion into a practical course of action.

A homeless man, bundled against the cold, solicits money on Fifth Avenue in New York City.

According to information supplied by the *Homeless Information Exchange*, action begins and results occur when individuals look for creative ways to help.

In Minnesota, for example, The Alliance of the Streets, an organization of poor and homeless persons, started a job program that has grown into a small business. The group borrowed money from the shelter where they lived and then advertised services such as cleaning and lawn care. Their business then grew to include painting, roofing, and car repair. Local churches provided funds for purchasing necessary equipment. Workers earn at least five dollars an hour.

A homeless woman arranges her possessions in front of her makeshift tent at the Phoenix Homeless Shelter. City officials estimate there are nearly seven thousand homeless people in the Phoenix area. Phoenix has a warm climate and attracts many homeless people.

In New York City, the Cooper Square Development Center purchased a building from the city for eleven thousand dollars. Then they borrowed money from state funds to rehabilitate it into cooperative apartments for twenty-two homeless families. Rent is controlled so that it cannot exceed the amount provided by welfare checks. Residents own the building and are responsible for its maintenance.

In Tucson, Arizona, private citizens from the Primavera Foundation, an agency that works with homeless families, organized to study the causes of homelessness. The foundation purchased a condemned motel and hired a group of homeless men to convert it into twenty small apartments for mentally-ill homeless persons. The men learned the necessary skills through on-the-job training. Later, the newfound skills helped them find work and permanent housing. Rental income from the apartments now supports the foundation.

Many people believe these examples make an important point. Citizens can take care of their own—especially those at the bottom. They do so, however, by working together with those who need help. Private citizens can provide the means, and then show the homeless the way to help themselves.

CHAPTER TWO

Street Children

The National Network of Runaway and Youth Services based in Washington, D.C., estimates the number of runaway children to be 1 to 1.5 million nationally. In Los Angeles alone, about 8,000 to 10,000 runaway kids come into contact with the county's service department each year.

Covenant House, a shelter for runaway kids near Times Square in New York City, provides street kids with a way and the means to help themselves. Founder and director Father Bruce Ritter, a Catholic priest, has taken in over 100,000 street kids during the last twenty years. He has since opened similar shelters in Canada, Texas, Florida, Louisiana, and South America.

He has done most of his work, however, in New York City, where the population of homeless persons (70,000 to 90,000) is the highest in the nation and where many homeless children live. According to the National Coalition for the Homeless, 20,000 children under eighteen years of age live on the streets of New York City.

"Kids don't survive very long on the street—at least in any recognizably human way," says Father Ritter. They lose their identities fast. Personalities fade. Characters dissolve. Even their looks change rapidly after just a few weeks.

"Kids come to Covenant House," he said, "because they have no place to go. The problem for all of them is very simple: Where am I going to sleep tonight? Or eat tonight? Who will take care of me tonight?"

But as Father Ritter wrote in his moving book, *Sometimes God Has a Kid's Face*, deeper still is the question "Who will love me and care about me?"

On the run

This new breed of homeless children is running. They run from rich families and from poor families. Many leave big houses, swimming pools, personal computers, and stereo equipment behind. Others leave crowded tenements, rats and disease, drunken parents, and screaming babies.

They want freedom. Some want freedom from family rules and regulations; others want freedom from abusive homes and families, physical and sexual violence, alcoholic parents, fighting, neglect, the demands of school, or drug problems. Teens who are caught in these struggles often see no choice but running. Even younger children escape to the streets when they can no longer function in their homes.

Many runaways arrive at Covenant House because they need help. Some may even know they deserve it—like one little lady who was only eleven years old when she turned up at Father Ritter's door.

"'A lady should never get this dirty,'" she said, standing there "with a quiet, proud dignity," recalled Father Ritter.

Her face and hands were smeared, and her clothes were torn and soiled. "My brothers are hungry," she said, clutching the hands of the eight- and nine-year-old boys. "Our parents beat us a lot," she said. "We had to leave." Then the dirty little girl asked Father Ritter if she could take a shower. They had lived on the street for two weeks.

Two weeks on the street is a long time. Three months on the street is a very long time. "Six months is forever," said Father Ritter. And a year? "Then they're just breathing in and out but dead inside. The poison works quickly."

The U.S. Department of Health and Human Services estimates that of the one million children in the United States who run away from home each year, 57 percent are products of a divorce; 16 percent have never known their fathers; 25 percent have been in mental institutions, and 48 percent have attempted suicide at least once.

Today's runaways are different from those of four or five years ago, according to Gary Yates, director of a program for youth at Children's Hospital in Los Angeles. They are younger than runaways of the past; 40 percent are age fifteen or younger. Many have never known what it is to be a child.

Most people think of a runaway as a kind of Huckleberry Finn,

Runaway teenagers hang out on street corners in big cities across the United States. There, many are lured into a life of drugs and prostitution. Because these teenagers need money to survive on the streets, they are easy prey for pushers and pimps.

Nearly 1.5 million runaway children are living on America's streets. Some run away from abusive homes or pursue a life of drugs and crime. But regardless of why these children run, they find that life on the streets is difficult for most, impossible for many. Some homeless children end up beaten, battered, or hooked on drugs.

cutting school and rafting down the river in search of adventure, said Yates. "They forget about Huck Finn's father being a chronic alcoholic who beat him near death every chance he got," he points out.

Many runaways who pour into New York City, Hollywood or San Francisco, California, and Fort Lauderdale, Florida, are children from dysfunctional families. Alcoholism, drug addiction, gambling, workaholism, sexual abuse, and emotional and physical neglect are *normal* in the homes of these families.

"Most of the kids we see have been hurt, and I mean really damaged," said Jed Emerson, director of Diamond Youth Shelter in San Francisco. "They don't trust the system, and they certainly don't trust adults."

Once these kids are on the streets, there is no place they can turn to for help. Workers in the child-welfare system claim they cannot find foster homes that will take these troubled kids. Officials of mental-health services say they cannot deal with the kids' emotional problems until the kids are treated for drug abuse. And substance-abuse clinics are overcrowded. Many kids are on waiting lists at treatment centers in major cities.

The reasons behind homelessness

How do these troubled kids get this way? Why do parents "throw away" their own children? Why do the kids themselves flee from their own flesh and blood?

A recent study conducted by the University of Connecticut showed that 86 percent of runaways at a Toronto shelter had been physically or sexually abused at home. Many of these same kids usually continue to be sexually-abused on the streets. Father Ritter said, "I have never met a young prostitute—boy or girl—who did not start out as a runaway."

When children are sexually abused in their own homes, many family members may be unable to deal with it. Some parents refuse to listen, or blame the children for "asking for it." Those same parents may have been abuse victims themselves. As the cycle repeats itself in the younger generation, these parents cannot or will not stop it. Some ignore it. Some throw the kids out.

Not all throwaway kids are victims of sexual abuse. Some are unwanted. They are told point-blank that they cost too much to take care of or that the mother or father is just plain sick of the hassle of parenting.

In some cases, it is the parents, rather than the children, who leave home. The children simply come home to empty houses. A single parent takes off with a boyfriend or girlfriend, abandoning the children.

Some kids are running away from foster homes, which may be worse than the homes they were taken from. One social worker reported that one of his clients had been in fifty-two foster homes. Life is challenging enough even for a child who is loved and cared for, but when a foster home becomes a network of lies, abuse, and neglect, some kids take off. They do not always know where they are going, but they may feel that anyplace is better than where they are.

First night alone

Sharon, sixteen, was a runaway. One night she found herself alone on the street, a small bag of belongings in one hand and a few dollars in her pocket. Her heroin-addicted mother had just kicked her out.

Earlier in life she had lived in a foster home for a time, but the adults there abused drugs, as her mother did. Sharon took off. Later she came to the attention of a social worker. Now she is living at a shelter in Massachusetts, getting counseling, and trying to recover her life.

For years, the United States has been in a fog over what to do with kids like Sharon. They are not criminals. They are referred to as status-offenders. They skip school, run away, create havoc, but they do not actually break the law. Even those who do break the law by doing drugs and selling their bodies are difficult to deal with. They are different from hardened adult criminals. They are children.

Once these kids come to the attention of the authorities, no one wants to be responsible for them. ''There's a general failure of the social-service system to deal with runaway and homeless youth,'' says June Bucy, executive director of the National Network of Runaway and Youth Services. These are not the kids whose faces you see on

Owning a pair of decent shoes can be a major problem for children living on the streets. Other major problems include finding food and a place to sleep.

milk cartons. "No one has reported these kids missing," she says. "No one is looking for them. And no one wants them when they are found."

Kids like Sharon are hungry for affection, direction, and attention. This makes them easy prey for the pimps and pushers who hang around the bus stations and train terminals waiting for runaways to arrive.

Survival sex

According to a news report in *USA Today,* "one in three [runaways] is lured into prostitution within forty-eight hours of leaving home."

"First, they will probably be raped," said Vikki Balet, director of Children of the Night, a social agency in Hollywood, California. A runaway who has been raped will not usually seek help right away. Most are afraid of being exposed. To deal with the guilt and pain, they turn to drugs. Then the pimps and con men move in and offer them comfort; before they know it, they are working in a prostitution ring.

Some of the runaways are as young as nine. For these children, the streets are especially cruel. To survive at all, they need each other.

Those who avoid prostitution look after one another, share food, and sleep fitfully in condemned buildings called "squats."

Street kids are easy to recognize. Hollow eyes, bleeding scabs, roughened skin, and matted hair are the telltale signs of fear, drug and alcohol abuse, too little sleep, and chronic undereating. When they get too hungry, too lonely, and too tired, even the most determined give in to "survival sex." Survival sex is the term used to describe various forms of sexual exploitation, including prostitution and pornography.

Police reports from major cities estimate that 90 percent of runaway youths who remain on the streets for several weeks end up giving sex in exchange for a bed and a meal.

Abused and battered

The cost of survival sex, however, is high. Many kids pay with their lives. Some are repeatedly raped, cut and battered, then left for dead. Older men—twenty-eight to thirty years old—keep some of the girls for awhile, then throw them out when the girls reach eighteen or nineteen.

Still others risk a slow death by contracting AIDS. A 1988 study by the U.S. Centers for Disease Control found that 13 percent of a sample of 835 young prostitutes from seven cities in the United States tested positive for AIDS.

For many street kids, these statistics are meaningless. "I'm going to die one way or the other on the street, so why worry about AIDS?" one said.

The kids may not worry. But some counselors and other professionals do. And kids who have been on the street for three or four years are often glad to come in contact with them.

Many counselors are involved with rescuing kids from the perils of survival sex. For example, each year, staff counselors from Children of the Night counsel hundreds of teens involved in prostitutional pornography in Southern California, a major center of pornography.

Eighty percent are recovered from the streets. Other centers around the United States report similar success rates. According to one counselor, once these kids get off the streets, they usually stay off.

Life on the needle

Tim was a street kid who had left a comfortable middle-class home at age thirteen to chase drugs. In 1970, Tim came to Father Ritter's apartment barely able to walk. He was a skinny, sixteen-year-old, black-haired, blue-eyed "speed freak" who "lived any way he

Buyers make drug deals on a street in New York City. Cocaine, pills, and heroin are sold through car windows. Unfortunately, many of the nation's homeless children become hopelessly hooked on drugs to relieve the pressure of their difficult lives. To get money to buy these drugs, street kids often resort to prostitution and other crimes.

Father Bruce Ritter of Covenant House in New York City talks with President George Bush and a homeless teenager. Father Ritter has taken in over 100,000 street kids during the last twenty years.

could," recalled Father Ritter. He lived "anyplace he could, pouring his life out daily through the hollow point of a needle."

Most mornings he was so weak and depressed he appeared almost dead. Father Ritter had to dress him—socks, shirt, pants—because Tim was unable to do it for himself.

Despite Ritter's care, the sly teen still managed to slip out and get high. Then one night Tim came back, flashed a wide, fake smile, went to his room, and swallowed thirty sleeping pills. "He didn't die, though he wanted to," said Ritter.

After that episode, Father Ritter had Tim evaluated at one of the major New York medical centers at which a research program in Methedrine (speed) addiction was underway. On a scale of one to ten, Ritter said the doctors and counselors all gave Tim a zero chance to make it.

Ritter and his friends continued to stay close to Tim as many hours as they could. Then, slowly, a miracle began to happen. Little by little, Tim began to change. First he managed to survive one whole day without drugs, then three days, and then suddenly a whole week went by without shooting up. Tim, Father Ritter, and his friends celebrated his victory. "You know, Bruce," Tim said that night, "I think I might live."

That summer, some of Ritter's friends enrolled Tim in a youth camp. They feared the worst. Instead Tim chopped wood, painted, learned to water ski, and developed a deep love for the forest and mountains. He also gained thirty pounds, and muscles appeared on his slender body for the first time ever!

That fall he enrolled in one of New York's best high schools. Gradually, Tim came out of the shadows. His mind started working again. In fact, he graduated—with honors!

To celebrate, Father Ritter, Tim and Tim's parents, with whom he had been reunited that year, had dinner together. Tim said it was the happiest day of his life. "I think it was mine, too," said Father Ritter.

However, Ritter added, "For every Tim, there are a dozen or twenty Johns, Marks, Marys, Bills, Cindys, who never come in out of the darkness, who can't tear free from their vices."

But the work of Covenant House, Children of the Night, Diamond Youth Shelter, and others goes on—despite the dropouts. Bruce Ritter and his 100 volunteers continue to open their doors to thousands of young people each year. Teachers, doctors, lawyers, retired businesspeople, nurses, grandparents, engineers, and all kinds of people help full-time. "They each promise to commit at least a full year," says Ritter. "I am inordinately proud of them, and I love them very much."

CHAPTER THREE

Life in a Shelter

Life in a private shelter—even a caring place like Covenant House—is not easy. And a public shelter is often as bad as the street.

In New York City, for example, thousands of children are housed in family shelters. In the Bronx, New York, homeless families set up camp in a city-run shelter that is little more than an enormous gymnasium. Eight rows of 210 cots and cribs are spread across the bare floor.

Thousands more children live in welfare hotels in New York City. These hotels are not suitable for young children. They are known for prostitutes, drug abusers, cockroaches, and rats. Ironically, the landlords of the roach-infested hotels receive up to eighteen hundred dollars from the city for each family's monthly rent.

The situation is similar in Washington, D.C. Families often live in run-down, filthy hotels. The landlords of these hotels, however, are well paid for providing these "homes." They receive as much as twenty-four hundred dollars a month per family for one room without kitchen appliances.

The locations of shelters and welfare hotels in New York City, Washington, D.C., and in other cities across the nation pose additional problems. Most are situated in dingy downtown areas where it is dangerous to be outside after dark. There is little privacy and almost no space for children to play.

The plight of the homeless is receiving more media attention than ever before. Journalists are writing about the homeless, and reporters are interviewing them for television newscasts. This media attention has spurred many major American cities to try to provide more and better shelters for those in need.

In New York, for example, the National Coalition for the Homeless reported that twenty thousand youngsters roamed the city streets in 1985. In response, Mayor Ed Koch committed the city to renovating four thousand apartments yearly for poor families.

City officials are also trying to persuade landlords to let the homeless live in empty apartments in exchange for a four-thousand-dollar cash bonus.

In Boston, six family shelters opened between 1983 and 1985. Staff members are becoming more sensitive to the needs of homeless children. So each of these shelters provides a mental-health or other health-care professional specializing in children's issues.

Massachusetts also offers people on welfare vouchers that they can use to receive a safe, sanitary room for up to ninety days.

In Los Angeles, a sixteen-bed center funded by the county offers a free room and meals to mothers with dependent children. While the women live at the center, officials save their checks and food stamps until there is enough money and food stamps for each woman to get a place of her own.

In Chicago, the Salvation Army's emergency shelter lodge brings in public school teachers each day to tutor the children. The lodge also provides free medical care and senior-citizen "foster grand-parents" to help parents with their children.

Following is a look at three different shelters in three different American cities and the effects they had on three young people who lived in them.

Portland, Oregon

Jill ran away from home at age fourteen. She had been molested by her father when she was a child. She is an alcoholic and a drug abuser. And she had been in and out of jail—until she enrolled in

Living conditions at many of the nation's welfare hotels are not fit for human beings. Landlords of these rat-infested hotels often receive large sums from the government for each family living there. A child who grows up in these conditions is more susceptible to ill-health.

the Girls' Emancipation Program in Portland. "If I hadn't come here," said Jill, "I would have exploded. I didn't feel anything when I was living on the streets. I just shut off my feelings."

Jill appeared to be getting in touch with her feelings again, however, after being in the program and living at the YWCA for some time. Even her room reflects her newfound self-respect. Stuffed animals sit next to each other in a row. Cosmetics are lined up neatly on the desk, and blankets are carefully folded on the bed.

Why did Jill run away? She was searching for love and security, she admitted. She thought she had found them in a man who was ten years older than she. But when he asked her to ''prove'' her love by becoming a prostitute in Portland's worst neighborhood, her downward spiral began. ''That's how it starts,'' she said, older and wiser now.

Jill hopes to be independent some day—and to stay off the streets permanently. She wants to take classes at the local community college, find an apartment, and get a job. She also started attending Alcoholics Anonymous meetings to deal with her drinking.

Homeless people gather around an oil-drum in a public shelter. Harsh winters sometimes force the homeless to flee to warmer climates. Many, however, brave the winter cold to stay in the cities.

Jill's chances for success, like those of other graduates of the program, are good. Nine of ten still have their jobs and apartments a year after leaving the program, claims Ruth Herman Wells, program director.

The Girls' Emancipation Program is a long-term (ninety days) shelter program that provides the girls of Portland's streets with an opportunity to cross from drug dependence to independence and a new life.

But residential treatment programs like this one are rare. More are needed. In Portland alone, some 200 girls are referred to this one program each year. But there are only thirty openings, according to Ms. Wells.

"These kids are close to the legal age [eighteen], so the state's Children's Services Division doesn't respond to them," she said. "It just doesn't have the resources and the options for the girls."

Port Orchard, Washington

Fifteen-year-old Billy lived in a shelter too, but his experience was different from Jill's. Billy and his mother and his younger brother, Joe, arrived in Port Orchard, Washington, with no place to live and almost no possessions—except Billy's cat. The family was placed in a county shelter.

"Billy held onto that cat as if it was the only thing he had in his life," said shelter director, Kathy Menz, in an interview with newsman Bob Greene. "In some ways, I guess it probably was."

But Billy soon found out that pets were not allowed in the shelter. So the cat had to leave. Billy could have the cat back, he was told, as soon as his mother found a place for them to live. Billy probably did not like the news. But he accepted it. He did not have much choice.

He did not have much choice about anything in his life. His family had lived in at least seven states. And when Billy was six, his dad deserted the family. "Billy blamed himself for his father having left," said Menz. "He felt responsible; he thought he must have done

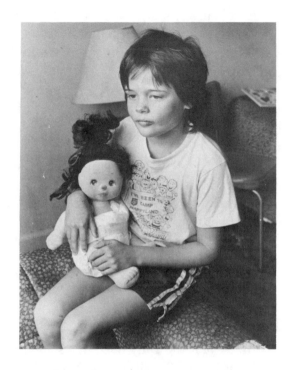

A homeless child stares vacantly into space. Homeless children face many hardships. For some, owning a special toy like a doll helps make life a little easier.

something wrong to make his dad run off. He hadn't, of course. It wasn't Billy's fault. But he felt it was.''

Then one day Billy met a man named Mack, who also lived in the county shelter with his family. Mack and Billy became friends. ''Billy was a nice, quiet kid,'' said Mack. ''He was a boy who worried whether other people would laugh at him.''

Since Billy never had a father to teach him how to do things, he felt awkward about throwing a baseball or a football. Mack showed him how, and he also encouraged Billy and told him that his life could turn out all right after all.

The friendship had a remarkable effect on Billy. Everyone at the shelter noticed it. ''You could actually see it,'' said Kathy Menz. But then everything changed when Billy's mother found a place for her family.

"When Billy heard he would be leaving the shelter, he was devastated," said Menz.

Here was a boy who never knew what it was like to have a dad. Someone finally came along to fill that role for Billy. "Then you tell him that he has to move on again . . . it was more than Billy could bear," added Menz.

One Sunday before they moved, Billy went upstairs and hanged himself in a closet. "I don't think he wanted to go on," said Menz. First he had to give up his cat and then his new friend. All that he had left was his cat's leash and he used that to end his life.

San Diego, California

Steve, seventeen, is off the streets, thanks to an emergency shelter in San Diego called The Storefront. But Steve was only twelve when he ran away from his home in San Diego. By the time he was fourteen, he was a mugger and drug dealer in New York.

"I was a totally different person," said Steve, as he reflected on his former life. He said that kids who knew him then would not recognize him now.

"Growing up in the eighties isn't easy," said Steve. "If you're a virgin at thirteen, you're an idiot. If you're not going around beating up someone and waving a [gang] color, you're a wimp. If you don't do drugs, you're not cool."

Steve is a product of the eighties. He is still working through his problems, but he is committed to getting well. "My dad spent thousands of dollars to keep me in programs," said Steve, "but The Storefront is worth more than all of them, and it's free. They do it with love. It's like family."

At The Storefront, kids like Steve live together under adult supervision. They sleep *in* three nights, *out* seven, in three and out seven, until they qualify for Phase II, when they can stay in for ninety consecutive nights.

The shelter provides twenty teens with a clean, safe, and nurturing

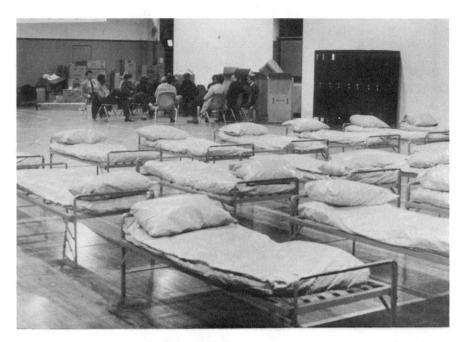

Many shelters, such as this one in New York City, consist of beds or cots lined up in an armory. While these shelters provide warmth and companionship, they offer no privacy. Two hundred or more people often crowd together in similar shelters across the country.

place to stay, including a bed, meals, and necessary clothing. More emergency shelters like The Storefront are needed to serve the city's growing population of runaways and abandoned kids. There are some five hundred street kids in San Diego. Many have come from other parts of the country.

San Diego attracts runaways for many reasons. Some come because of the warm climate, the beach, and the easy access to drugs and alcohol on both sides of the California/Mexico border. Others drift south from Hollywood after being disillusioned or hurt by pornographers posing as film producers.

Still others are there because it is their hometown. They may have been kicked out by parents because of arguments over drugs or because of a family breakup.

Kids at The Storefront learn to take life one day at a time. In the morning, they have cold cereal and milk for breakfast; they are on their own for lunch; and dinner is brought in by volunteers.

Sandra McBrayer, a staff teacher, loves the kids at The Storefront and the kids love her. "You really care" is a phrase she hears again and again.

"My desire is to get these kids in here and make it interesting

Two residents of a shelter for homeless men in Newark, New Jersey, rest on beds in the basement of a former bank building. Such shelters are usually filled to capacity by early evening.

enough so they'll want to come back,'' she said. ''We're not doing structured high school work here. The kids aren't learning about Christopher Columbus and nouns and verbs, but they are learning about life and people, and more important, about themselves.''

McBrayer's one big rule is ''No guns, no knives, no weapons.'' People are often shocked by the kids' street talk, but McBrayer does not let it bother her. She says it is important to get the kids talking in any way they can—for now—or they may stop talking altogether. ''Weapons are inappropriate,'' she said confidently, ''not words.''

The most important thing is to reach the child within each runaway. They are looking for love and approval. McBrayer gives them both. One year she surprised her students with an Easter party. She brought in baskets; each child had a basket with his or her name on it. ''At first they didn't want to hunt for eggs. They said I was treating them like five-year-olds,'' she said. But when she turned them loose, they could not move fast enough.

These are kids who long for a real home and a caring family. Many, like Steve, turn to gangs, sex and drugs, and violence because they want to belong. They want to feel they matter in some way. A gang can give a homeless youth a sense of identity, importance, and protection.

But Sandra McBrayer believes there is hope. She and the staff have found a home for one boy with a terminal illness. They rescued another from an abandoned car where he lived alone and forgotten.

McBrayer located doctors and other health care professionals who agreed to provide medical treatment for the children. She is helping one girl acquire her credits for high school graduation. One boy has given up drugs because he "doesn't want to offend the staff."

"It's working," she said with a smile. "Maybe not as fast as we'd like it to, but what we're doing here is working. I have kids who are going for their high school equivalency, some who have jobs now and apartments of their own. And I meet with some once a week to help them finish their schooling. Imagine the pressure on these kids. Some work, care for a baby, study, and live alone—yet they want to learn. They want a better life."

CHAPTER FOUR

Schools for the Poor and Homeless

According to a report furnished by the U.S. Department of Education, over 70,000 homeless children are not attending school regularly.

However, the National Coalition for the Homeless estimates a much higher number than the Department of Education. The Coalition reports that between 166,000 and 266,000 homeless children are not attending school on a regular basis. Lack of transportation, transfer of health and school records, and requirements for permanent addresses were some of the obstacles reported.

Homeless parents and children often have personal reasons as well. They become discouraged by frequent moves, lack of money and clothes, short stays at temporary shelters, lack of day care, and problems with health care. All current research points to the same thing: special services and programs for homeless school-age children are desperately needed.

Many school districts and individual teachers took creative steps of their own. Classrooms specifically for the homeless were opened in some cities. In others, businesses, private citizens, and assertive teachers and parents started to change education for the poor.

New York has more children living in temporary housing than any other state. About half of these are school-age children. Until 1988, however, many of these children lived outside the central school district of New York City and were denied the opportunity to attend school.

For example, when a family was suddenly homeless and forced to live in a shelter or motel, the children's schooling was often interrupted. Sometimes the interruption lasted for months at a time. Neither their original schools nor the ones near the shelter or motel would accept them. Legally, they do not have to accept such students because the schools do not receive state financial aid for students without a permanent address.

In 1988, after a growing number of complaints and lawsuits on behalf of the children, the New York City Board of Regents came up with a remedy. The parents could select their children's school, and the school could not refuse them. Officials say this new rule has given homeless kids stability in at least one area of their lives—education.

Salt Lake City, Utah

Salt Lake City is one of the few major cities to open a classroom specifically for the homeless. Marilyn Treshow is the teacher who "makes learning fun," as one student put it.

Treshow, with help from the Salt Lake City School District and the Travelers Aid Society, opened her classroom for homeless school-age children in 1984. She teaches as few as three children or as many as thirty-five at a time. They range in age from five to eighteen.

"Many of these children," said Treshow, "have seen a lifetime of hurt." It is her desire to offer relief, at least during school hours.

The children in Treshow's class live temporarily in a cluster of five orange-and-white trailers that make up Salt Lake City's family shelter. Another shelter room serves as the School with No Name.

Some of the students are in school for a few months, others for

Teacher Marilyn Treshow reads to her students in her classroom for the homeless in Salt Lake City, Utah. In addition to teaching the children reading, writing, spelling, and math, Treshow also takes them on field trips.

only a few days. This changing population requires Treshow to use some special skills both to provide continuity and to let the kids know that their situation does not have to last forever.

Children are not the only ones who appreciate the School with No Name. "If it weren't for this school, my daughter would probably be way behind other kids when she goes back to regular school," said Rose, who came to Salt Lake City from Mexico looking for a job. "The homeless have been forgotten in so many areas. It makes the going easier to know that somebody else cares about your child's future."

Volunteer Ellen Woodward said, "I've taught in public schools before, but this is the only one I've ever seen where kids can't wait for the door to be unlocked so they can get in."

School begins at 8:00 a.m. Monday through Friday. Students learn and review basic skills in math and reading, writing, and spelling until noon. Then Treshow takes them on a field trip to a museum, the park, the zoo, or the planetarium.

Kids are kids, however, at this school as well as any other. The system is not perfect. There is the usual assortment of fighting and shouting, but Treshow has worked out an appealing program for restoring order and encouraging cooperation. She awards yellow tickets for good behavior. A child who earns twelve tickets receives a puzzle, a book, or a doll.

These are special treats to children who have almost nothing of their own. Most wear ill-fitting, donated clothing and shoes. And

Two children play in a neighborhood that looks more like a war zone. Many poor and homeless children must play games amid the rubble that constitutes their communities. Statistics prove that children like these will have a difficult time escaping the poverty that permeates their lives.

Few shelters or welfare hotels offer safe places for children to play. Many are located on muddy fields with broken glass and other trash. Inadequate food, housing, and clothing coupled with dangerous neighborhoods make the lives of these children painfully difficult.

many do not even have enough to eat. They receive sandwiches for lunch and sometimes only bread and jam for dinner.

The shelter's playground is a muddy field with broken glass and debris. Many of the children come to school sick, overtired, and dirty. Illness is frequent among homeless children in a shelter because they are together twenty-four hours a day. "If one gets the flu, half the class gets it," said Treshow.

But Treshow is not only concerned about the children's physical health. She also cares about their emotional well-being. To help them become more expressive, Treshow encourages them to fill out "How I'm Feeling" cards and place them in pockets by the bulletin board. Being able to write about how they feel can help homeless children ease the burden of carrying frightening emotions all alone.

San Diego, California

The brown wooden building on 15th Street looks like an old warehouse from the outside. At one time it was. But today the fan belts and other car parts that once filled the warehouse are gone. In their place are desks and bulletin boards and bookshelves and easels—and lots of kids. This school is part of San Diego's Summit Schools, a system created for students with special needs.

"I like being a part of this system," said teacher Sally Wooten. "I enjoy working with them [the homeless]. After fourteen years as a high school teacher, this is something entirely different for me."

Wooten said there are many advantages to this type of special classroom. For example, the parents must sign their children in and out each day. This allows parents and teachers to become acquainted and to work together for the children's best interests. Each child is also evaluated personally on entering the school and then encouraged to progress at his or her own pace.

Students receive individual attention in reading, math, and other subjects. Wooten works with students at her desk while other students receive help from teachers' aides and volunteers.

Many homeless parents worry about how their children will get an education. According to one report, nearly eighty thousand homeless children are not attending school regularly.

One father told Wooten that he wishes his kids could continue at the school even after the family leaves the nearby shelter. He said that this is the place where his children opened up and blossomed.

Wooten made the point that older children find it more difficult to adjust to homelessness than younger children do. "The younger group is not as disturbed by the family's circumstances as the older ones," said Wooten. "They're fine as long as they have what they need and know we're glad to see them each morning."

In a classroom like this, however, there is a lot of uncertainty. The teacher may not know that a family is moving until its name is removed from the daily census list from the shelter. One morning they are gone. Many do not have the chance to say good-bye.

Despite the uncertainty, Sally Wooten is hopeful. "I definitely have hope," she said. "It's sad to see them leave, but it usually means that better times are ahead for these kids. Their families have work and a place to go, and that makes us feel good."

Making a difference

The requirements for escaping long-term poverty in the United States are straightforward—according to a report published by a group of scholars and government officials.

Finish high school, get *any* job (even at the minimum wage), and stay in the labor market. Get married as an adult and stay married. These are demanding tasks, claims the report, but not superhuman.

One survey completed in the 1970s showed that "just earning a high school diploma helped keep all but 0.6 percent of adult men and all but 2 percent of adult women out of poverty." That says a lot for the value of receiving an education.

According to a study by a group of scholars and government officials, this child must finish high school to get a decent-paying job and escape poverty. But going to school requires stability. Many homeless people move from shelter to shelter, and their children often go without an education.

But not every child hears or believes these statistics. More needs to be done to bring kids from the streets, shelters, and slums into classrooms.

But meanwhile, some children *are* learning and growing and expressing themselves—even while surveys and reports and statistics are being compiled. They are changing their lives because of teachers like Marilyn Treshow, Sally Wooten, and others, who are proving everyday in their classrooms that even one person can make a difference!

CHAPTER FIVE

Homeless Children Speak Out

Children and teenagers become homeless for a variety of reasons. But all of them face severe problems in their attempts to survive in the streets. In order to gain a better understanding of the problems these children and teens face, a number of their personal stories are presented below. All of the stories are based on interviews at teen shelters in San Diego, California.

Seventeen-year-old Milt told reporters he wanted "to help others avoid his mistakes." He was snorting "crystal" (methamphetamine) at age thirteen and selling it to friends by age fourteen. He lived like a bum on the streets, sold drugs by day, and snorted up his profits at night. "I was dealing to a lot of guys from my area," said Milt, "but it just got old, real fast. It was awful." Milt has since kicked his drug habit at a local rehabilitation center.

Not all runaways are as easily reformed as Milt. Some find it difficult to escape the life they have created on the streets. Seventeen-year-old "Hollywood," for example, is now in a temporary shelter, but he is not ready to give up the streets.

He likes to play football and baseball, but there is not much time for sports when you are a homeless runaway. Most of the time, he is out on the streets doing anything he can to survive. He delivers packages containing illegal goods, arranges sexual favors for older men, and sells drugs.

"At times I want to be on the streets," Hollywood said, grinning. "I'm smart. I'm sneaky. I know where to go." He is thought of as a runaway, but actually he is part of the growing number of "throwaways." One day, after a bitter argument with his dad, he was ordered to pack up and leave.

"I've led a real lousy life," said Hollywood. "My dad's an alcoholic, and when I was seven one of my mom's boyfriends molested me."

Tina talked about her life on the streets. "It seems like you have to be really tough with everyone," she said. "You have to put up this big old front. Anyone that looks at you wrong, you think you have to threaten 'em. You have to act tough and coldhearted."

Then she talked about her life at the teen shelter. "I've calmed down a lot since I got into this program," she said. "When I first came I had this major acting problem. I used to steal and fight and kick people. Now I'm more mellow. I'm more me."

Eighteen-year-old Marty is a drug dealer. He started selling crystal at age fourteen, and his habit nearly destroyed his life. "There's a saying out here [on the streets]," he said, "that the only places drugs will get you is in jail or dead." Marty has nearly proven the saying in his own life. He has served time in jail, and he has nearly died twice.

Still children—inside

Homeless children live on America's streets and in back alleys, abandoned cars, community parks. They sleep on rooftops, in doorways, or in the street. By the time they are out there even a few months, many hit bottom. They deal drugs, drink too much, sell their bodies for a bed and a meal. Some want out of the street life. Others seem too far gone to care what happens next.

"I've had ulcers and often think of suicide," Sally said, brushing

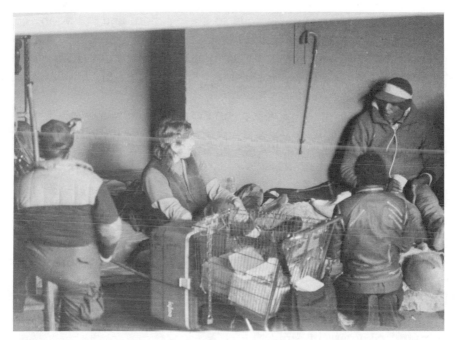

Homeless men pack their belongings into shopping carts on the San Francisco Civic Center loading dock. It is Thanksgiving Day and they are preparing to eat dinner at a local soup kitchen.

aside a strand of her blonde hair. "Because when you're away and alone you have to act hard to protect yourself and survive. The longer you're on the streets, the harder it is to survive because you start running out of friends."

Danny carries a knife. "Most of us do," he said proudly. "You've got to—for protection. Or you'll get mugged or raped or beaten up."

"I've supported myself doing off-the-wall jobs like . . . selling drugs, but I never prostituted myself because that's degrading," added Sally. "I sleep in boats, bathrooms, parking lots, beaches—wherever." Now Sally sleeps at a youth shelter because she's sick of street life.

Fifteen-year-old Leila's mother just got out of jail. Leila does not want to end up like that. "I want to go to school and get a job and go to college someday. I'm tired of living on the streets," she said. "I've gone from having everything to nothing in one day. Every time I get something of my own, somebody rips me off and I have to start all over again."

Nineteen-year-old Vic tried to get off the streets by moving in with an older man. When the older man started doing drugs, Vic left fast. "It's not easy to find people you can trust," said Vic. "I was a criminal for awhile. I did whatever I had to do to survive. Most of the stuff I'm not too proud of. But I don't want that life anymore. I'm back in school now, and I'm gonna get my high school equivalency."

Jenny, thirteen, left home because her mother abused her. "I always said I'd never sell my body for a meal," she said hesitantly. "But there comes a time when you ain't got no money and no food and no place to go, and that's all that's left to do. I wish I could be a child again, but it's too late. Now I just want to finish school and get a job, and someday when I have kids of my own, I'm gonna love 'em and take care of 'em."

For most runaways and street kids, recovery is a long and painful journey. Seventeen-year-old Scott told a newspaper reporter that he started smoking marijuana when he was thirteen and selling drugs at age fourteen. He dropped out of eight rehabilitation programs. In 1988, Scott became desperate for a new start.

"I was so into crystal, it changed my personality. I would go out looking for trouble," said Scott, who also told his story to warn others about the dangers of taking drugs. "Finally, I just told my ma that if I got high again, I would die."

A poor start

Some homeless kids seemed doomed almost from the start. "I grew up in the projects," said Wes, referring to his early years in a welfare settlement in the South. "I just hung around the streets and watched people do certain things. That's how I learned what I know,'' he said proudly.

Wes sees a counselor at a local mental health center—when he feels like it, which is not very often. Back on the street, he just ''hangs out.''

Some girls hang out on the streets—and hanging out causes problems. The most common problem is getting pregnant. ''When I was fifteen,'' said Ethel, ''I thought you couldn't get pregnant until you were eighteen. Now I know different. Boy, do I!'' she said.

Gordy is a wise guy. He does not agree with the youths who want to go back to school and get jobs. He says he can make more money dealing drugs. ''I ain't working no forty hours a week for a hundred

A suspected gang member is searched by Los Angeles police for drugs and weapons. Many homeless children turn to gangs for companionship, only to find the same violence and abuse they found at home.

This child holds a blackboard listing tasks she must complete for school. Realizing that children need structure in their lives, many schools and shelters schedule daily activities.

dollars or a hundred fifty dollars when I can work the streets for maybe fifteen minutes and come back with a thousand dollars."

Carlos sees it another way. "Man, I went two, three years without working. I just hung out drinking beer, smoking reefer. Then I got a job and I couldn't handle it. I hated having to get up in the morning and go someplace where all they do is push and shove. So I went back to the streets. Now I can't stand the streets no more," he said wistfully.

"I see these old guys walking around, all bent over, and I wonder if that's gonna be me in another twenty years—if I live that long. I get scared. I want something better. I don't even know what that means. But I want something better,'' he said, staring out the window.

Something better

Something better is available. Milt and Scott and Jenny and Vic know that now from personal experience. There are people and places and services that care about these young people and want to help them help themselves. However, there are not enough such places. Volunteers and social workers have enormous workloads, and there is almost never enough money to meet the needs. But homeless kids

Maria Tanco, left, claps after her daughter, Tatiana, completes a puzzle at the Great Northern Daycare Center in the Regency Hotel in New York City. Mental health aide Joyce Floyd looks on happily.

are finding their way back. For some, it is the first good taste of life they have ever known.

Wendell, eighteen, is one example. He is now in a recovery program. He said he thinks kids do drugs and sex to make friends, and to forget the stuff that bothers them—like abuse and fear and not being loved. "When you do drugs," he said, "you can sell 'em and then you have money in your pocket all the time. And you can have a car and girls, and if you're in a gang you got protection. Somebody's always looking out for you—unless you cross 'em, of course. Then they're looking *for* you."

"Being in a gang is exciting, and it gives you power," said Wendell's brother, Louis. "But the thing I don't like about it is it's limited. You got to stay with the same group all the time. You can't go into another gang's territory. I'm in this program," he said, "because I want to get a job and a place of my own and finish school. I want to make a better life."

Johnny, seventeen, chose drugs and he chose friends who were on drugs. In less than a year, he dropped out of school and left home. "But I couldn't take it out there," Johnny confessed. "Maybe I wasn't tough enough. I don't know. But I couldn't take it. It's hell on the streets. Some nights I thought I was gonna die. Probably I was," he added softly.

"Then I met this guy who told me about a shelter that helped teens, and so I went there and they helped me and they called my family. I got into a drug rehab program. My whole family went," he said proudly. "I'm gettin' my high school credits now. Someday I wanna be a teacher or maybe a social worker. I'm not sure. Kids are our future. I want them to know they can have something better if they want it bad enough."

CHAPTER SIX

Who Will Save the Children?

Children are our future, the hope of our land, the leaders of tomorrow. Children are our most precious resource. Teachers, parents, politicians, and ministers preach the value of our youth from podiums and pulpits across our nation. But do they mean it? "No civilized society would treat its children like we treat ours and then say children are our best resource," said Ira Schwartz of the Center for Youth Policy at the University of Michigan.

Federal and state policies and funds for children's services do not meet the needs of America's homeless children. And less money is being set aside for these young people each year. One program helping homeless children, called Aid to Families with Dependent Children, has been cut by 1.7 billion dollars since 1980.

Steps toward change

How do we bring about change? How do we save the children? What can one person do? One way to tackle any problem—particularly a problem of such size—is to break it into manageable pieces. Then look at the pieces.

Trevor Ferrell is one example of a person who saw a need and looked for a way to get involved. In 1983, he was an eleven-year-old boy living with his family in Philadelphia, Pennsylvania. One night in December of that year, Trevor saw a news story about homeless people in his city.

"Do they really live like that here in America?" Trevor asked his dad. "They're out there in the cold and snow right now. Where do they eat? How do they stay alive?"

He began to think of a way he could help. First, he coaxed his parents into driving him into the city, where he gave a yellow blanket and a pillow to a man huddled on a subway steam grate. The next night Trevor returned with food and clothing for others. And he returned the night after that and the night after that.

Weeks later, after the Ferrells had emptied their own pantry and closets, they approached friends and customers at Mr. Ferrell's store and fellow members of their church. People began to respond. They wanted to do something about the growing problem of homelessness in Philadelphia.

One young boy's accomplishments

Before long, Trevor's campaign made the newspapers and television newscasts in Philadelphia. Soon after, he became known throughout the United States. People were amazed at what one young boy could accomplish.

Today Trevor Ferrell is no longer a small boy; he is a teenager who is over six feet tall. Just as he has grown since 1983, so has his program for the homeless. Street people are now served from three food vans, and his mother runs a thrift shop. In addition, a three-story former hotel (now named "Trevor's Place") houses up to forty-two homeless men, women, and children.

Trevor's Campaign for the Homeless began as one boy's dream of doing something for people in need. He did not back away because the problem was too big. And he did not try to tackle the entire problem. He started with one blanket and one pillow for one man. Today Trevor's Campaign for the Homeless, directed by his father, is a

Trevor Ferrell was eleven years old when he began passing out food and blankets to the homeless in Philadelphia. Trevor's compassion gave rise to a campaign to help the homeless in Philadelphia.

750,000 dollar operation with fourteen employees and more than eight hundred volunteers.

Hope in Five Points

In another part of the United States, Ray and Marilyn Stranske also saw a need in their community. They wanted to help homeless families in a neighborhood called Five Points in Colorado find suitable places to live.

The challenge was great. Five Points is a crime-ridden neighborhood in Denver filled with junked cars, abandoned apartment buildings, and trash-packed yards. It is known as Denver's "Harlem" because of its resemblance to New York City's ghetto.

To anyone who drives through the community, it may seem beyond hope. But not to Ray and Marilyn Stranske. The couple founded Hope Community in 1980 for the purpose of reclaiming and fixing up abandoned apartment buildings and neglected houses for homeless and poor families. By the end of 1988, the Stranskes had helped renovate homes for 107 families.

Laura, a twenty-nine-year-old mother and C.J., her eighteen-month-old son, are among the fortunate new residents. When Laura arrived in Denver after her marriage ended, she stayed with relatives for awhile. Then, after her job search had failed, in desperation she turned to a shelter for the homeless. Later, Laura went on welfare so she could get a small basement apartment for herself and her son. But rent took most of her welfare check, and she soon became frantic wondering how she could go on.

One miraculous day she learned about Hope Community. Since then, her life has completely turned around. With the help of Hope Community staff members, Laura has received job training, the ability to give her son a home, and student aid so she can continue her education.

Model programs

On the west coast, San Diego, California, received recognition in a report in *Fortune* magazine for its "exemplary shelter system funded entirely by private money."

The St. Vincent de Paul/Joan Kroc Center is one of the most well-known examples. This Center is the dream of founder and director, Father Joe Carroll, who has been serving the homeless in San Diego since 1983.

The Center offers qualified families and individuals long-term housing (up to a year or more), food, clothing, private living quarters within the building, recreational activities, schooling, job counseling, and day care. The Center has won international recognition and is now considered a model for other cities.

About eighty miles north of San Diego, in San Juan Capistrano, George and Betty Wakeling provide shelter of a different kind. Their foster-care program, Concept 7, focuses on safe housing for children who have been physically or sexually abused. Some of these children are left homeless when parents are imprisoned or considered unfit.

Treating homeless children like their own

"We started taking children into our home," said George Wakeling, "when our own children were growing up." For several years, the couple had twelve to fifteen children living with them at one time. Then, after six years, they decided to go back to school to get their degrees and licenses so they could operate a center professionally.

Today Concept 7 is a fully licensed, private foster-care program, providing a wide range of emergency-to-long-term housing and care for boys and girls from birth through age seventeen.

Affiliated with Concept 7 is The California Family Center. The Center provides a second division of foster care for children who have suffered more trauma.

"When I use the word *trauma*," said Wakeling, "I mean they are acting out their anger. They're mad at their families. They're confused about what love is. And they don't trust people.

"Just last week a little two-year-old came to us who had been abandoned. Even though that child is only two, he remembers some of that trauma."

Eleven Concept 7 homes are staffed twenty-four hours a day with professional child-care workers in three counties to meet the special needs of these hurting children. "Some of these children," said Wakeling, "have been sexually abused by members of their own family for over half their lifetime."

George Wakeling also talked fondly about his wife and partner, Betty Wakeling. "None of what I have done would have been possible without my wife. She has been by my side from the beginning and is an inspiration to me." Also at his side were the Wakelings' children, all now working on the Concept 7 staff in some capacity.

The Wakelings' dream for the future is to "build a 100-bed campus with our own school. Then my wife and I hope someday to stop doing administrative work and to simply live at the camp and be grandma and grandpa to these kids."

What can *you* do?

Many people believe volunteer citizens could do much to aid homeless children. Following is a list of suggestions for people interested in getting involved in helping the homeless:

Find out what is going on in your community. To start with, you can write to the National Coalition for the Homeless, 105 East 22nd Street, New York, NY 10010, for a booklet listing the names of agencies in your state that work for the homeless. You could also call your local newspaper or check with a librarian for the names of shelters and other groups who provide care for homeless children.

Trevor Ferrell offers a hot drink to a homeless man in Philadelphia.

Call one or two to start with and find out what they need and how a person your age could contribute.

Contribute basic necessities. The population of a homeless shelter changes frequently, so there is always a need for basics such as food, clothing, blankets, soap, toothpaste, toothbrushes, hairbrushes and combs, and other personal-care items.

Round up the support of friends and family. Children in foster-care and residential-treatment programs would welcome posters and pictures for their bedroom walls, some pretty spring flowers for the yard, a fresh coat of paint on the walls. These are ideal projects for families, church youth groups, or scout troops.

Volunteers receive food donations that will feed many homeless people on Thanksgiving Day. Because the government cannot bear the entire responsibility for feeding and housing the poor, citizens have stepped in to help.

Raise money to donate to a shelter or program for homeless children. One thirteen-year-old boy asked the kids at his birthday party to collect donations from neighbors in order to buy Christmas presents for homeless children.

Be a friend. Become a pen pal with a homeless child in foster care in another city. You might donate a book or a toy to a particular child, or become part of a storytelling team at a shelter with a group from your church or scout troop. Many homeless children are as starved for real friendship as they are for a home of their own.

Share what you know. Become informed. Send away for booklets and pamphlets from the National Coalition for the Homeless and share them with friends. If you suspect or know of someone who is threatening to run away, give him or her the telephone number of a crisis hotline. Here is one for Covenant House in New York: 1-800-999-9999. This help line is open and toll-free twenty-four hours a day.

Working with homeless children and their families may seem difficult or overwhelming because their needs are so great. But it does not have to be discouraging. Everyone can do something. Remember how Trevor Ferrell's first gesture to one man turned into a full-time project to help homeless men, women, and children.

The choice is ours. We can ignore the problem or we can take that first step, however small, and find out for ourselves that one person *can* make a difference.

Suggestions for Further Reading

Michael J. Christensen, *City Streets, City People*. Nashville, TN: Abingdon Press, 1989.

William Dudley, ed., *Poverty: Opposing Viewpoints*. San Diego: Greenhaven Press, Inc., 1988

Stephenie Hollyman and Victoria Irwin, *We the Homeless: Portraits of America's Displaced People*. New York: Philosophical Library, 1988.

Jonathan Kozol, *Rachel and Her Children—Homeless Families in America*. New York: Crown Publishers Inc., 1988.

Mary Ellen Mark and Cheryl McCall, *Streetwise*. Philadelphia: University of Pennsylvania Press, 1988.

Tom Mathews, "Homeless in America: What Can Be Done?" *Newsweek*, March 21, 1988, pp. 57-58.

Milton Meltzer, *Poverty in America*. New York: William Morrow and Company, 1986.

F. Stevens Redburns and Terry F. Buss, *Responding to America's Homeless*. New York: Praeger Publishers, 1986.

David Whitman, "Hope for the Homeless," *U.S. News & World Report*, February 29, 1988, pp. 25-35.

Hank Whittemore, "We Can't Pay the Rent," *Parade* magazine, January 10, 1988, pp. 4-6.

Newsletters

These newsletters provide the public with information about the various aspects of homelessness.

Foodlines
published by Food Research
   and Action Center
1319 F St. NW
Washington, DC 20004
(202) 393-5060
($20 subscription)

Mental Health Law Project Update
2021 L St. NW
Washington, DC 20036
(202) 467-5730
($25 donation)

Safety Network
published by the National
   Coalition for the Homeless
1439 Rhode Island Ave. NW
Washington, DC 20005
(202) 659-3310
(donation requested)

Shelterforce
published by National Housing Institute
439 Main St.
Orange, NJ 07050
(201) 678-3110
(subscription: $15 individual,
   $25 organization)

Organizations to Contact

Contact the National Coalition for the Homeless for a full list of organizations for the homeless in various states.

Children's Defense Fund
122 C St. NW
Washington, DC 20001
(202) 628-8787

Clearinghouse on Homelessness Among Mentally Ill People (CHAMP)
8630 Fenton St., Suite 300
Silver Spring, MD 20910
(301) 588-5484

Homelessness Exchange
Community Information Exchange
1120 G St. NW, Suite 900
Washington, DC 20005
(202) 628-2990/2981

The National Coalition for the Homeless
1439 Rhode Island Ave. NW
Washington, DC 20005
(202) 659-3310

or

105 E. 22nd St.
New York, NY 10010
(212) 460-8110

National Low Income Housing Coalition
1012 14th St. NW, Suite 1006
Washington, DC 20005
(202) 662-1530

National Volunteer Hotline
1-800-HELP-664
Operated by the Community for
   Creative Non-Violence (CCNV)
425 2nd St. NW
Washington, DC 20001

Index

Acknowledgments

The author wishes to thank all the individuals and organizations whose expertise and photographs contributed to the writing of this book.

Susan Burris, Hillcrest School (Hillcrest Receiving Home for Abused Children), San Diego, California

Sandra McBrayer, teacher, The Storefront, San Diego, California

George Wakeling, Concept 7 and Branch Services for Children, San Juan Capistrano, California

National Coalition for the Homeless, Washington, D.C. and New York, New York

Aid for the Benefit of Children, New York, New York

Father Bruce Ritter, Covenant House, New York, New York

Sally Wooten, teacher, Harbor Summit School, San Diego, California

Everett McGlothlin, principal, Summit Schools, San Diego, California

Picture Credits

Photos supplied by Dixon and Turner Research
  Associates, Bethesda, MD.

Cover photo, Uniphoto
A/P Wide World Photos, 14, 21, 22, 32, 38, 42, 43, 57, 61
Jim Hubbard, 10, 12, 15, 17, 26, 27, 30, 37, 40, 49, 50, 52, 53,
  60, 69
Trevor's Campaign, 65, 68
UPI/Bettmann Newsphotos, 20, 59
George Wirt, 33
Don Wright, *The Miami News*, 44
Dale Wittner/People Weekly/© 1987 Time Inc., 48

About the Author

Karen O'Connor is an award-winning author. She has over 300 magazine articles, two films, and twenty published books to her credit, including *Contributions of Women: Literature*, *Maybe You Belong in a Zoo*, and the best-selling *Sally Ride and the New Astronauts*.

She is an instructor for The Institute of Children's Literature and teaches writing workshops for the University of California and other adult education programs in the state. She has served as a national language arts consultant for the Glencoe Publishing Company and is a frequent guest speaker at schools and professional groups throughout the country.